W9-CSK-661

WALK ON WATER, PETE!

by Luis Palau

MULTNOMAH PRESS
Portland, Oregon 97266

*My special thanks to Mr. Fred Renich,
whose messages and personal concern
taught me to grow along with Peter.*

Scripture quotations in this book, unless otherwise
indicated, are from The New Testament in Modern English,
copyright J.B. Phillips 1958. Used by permission of the
Macmillan Company.

KJV—King James Version

RSV—Revised Standard Version, copyrighted 1946 and
1952 by the Division of Christian Education of the NCCC,
U.S.A., and used by permission.

Previously published under ISBN 0-8307-0286-5

Second Printing

©1981 by Luis Palau
Printed in the United States of America

All rights reserved. No part of this publication may be
reproduced, stored in a retrieval system, or transmitted,
in any form or by any means, electronic, mechanical,
photocopying, recording, or otherwise, without the
prior written permission of the publisher.

Library of Congress Cataloging in Publication Data

Palau, Luis, 1934-
  Walk on water, Pete!

  Reprint of the ed. published by G/L Regal Books,
Glendale, Calif.
    1. Christian life—1960-   2. Peter, Saint,
apostle. I. Title.
[BV4501.2.P27 1981]   248.4   80-39955
ISBN 0-930014-34-0 (pbk.)

CONTENTS

Redemption as Illustrated in the Life of Simon Peter

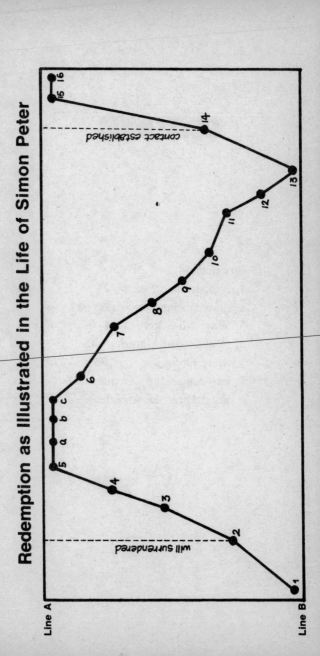

Line A is the level of mature, Spirit-controlled, Christian living. Redemption is that work of God whereby man is brought from the lower to the higher level; into the place where his life is dominated by the love of God, His glory and will. The well-being of others, as opposed to his old life where selfishness ruled.

Line B is the level of life where the dominant characteristic is selfishness. It is the plane of carnal living occupied by the unsaved and the carnal Christian.

1. Christ and Peter first meet. Christ proclaims, "thou art . . ." (conviction) and "thou shalt be . . ." (hope).
John 1:40-42

2. "Depart from me, Lord, for I am a sinful man." Peter sees something of his heart. Peter's salvation settled as he surrenders his will.
Luke 5:4-11

3. Peter walked on water at God's command. Obedience is faith in action.
Matthew 14:25-31

4. "Will you also leave me," Christ asks. Peter says, "Lord, who else should we go to?" He only will stick to Christ who has no one else to go to. Who has the answers for you?
John 6:48-69

5. "You are the Christ, the Son of the living God." (a) Christ is revealed and Peter is taught by the Spirit. (b) The promise of Christ to Peter is fulfilled as he says, "thou art Peter." (c) Peter's commission is made plain and enlarged.
Matthew 16:13-20

6. The Gospel now begins to be revealed as something diametrically opposite to human nature or reasoning. Peter shows he is not ready to take up his cross.
Matthew 16:21

7. Peter is rebuked for deciding he should build monuments for Christ, Moses, and Elijah on the mountain. A voice came out of the cloud, "This is my dearly loved Son in whom I am well pleased. Listen to him!" Peter, control your tongue.
Matthew 17:2-8

8. "How many times shall I forgive someone." Legalism. Quit counting, Peter.
Matthew 18:21,22

9. "What then shall I get?" Peter felt he deserved a reward for his spirituality.
Matthew 19:27

10. "Lord, you must never wash my feet." Peter protested. And Christ replied, "Unless you let me wash you, Peter, you cannot share my lot."
John 13:4-11

11. Christ tells Peter he will deny Him. John 13:36,37

12. Peter grabs the sword—carnal weapons.
John 18:10,11

13. The denial.
Luke 22:54-62

14. Peter called again and commissioned.
John 21:1-19

15. Exit Simon the Disciple; enter Peter the Apostle.
John 21:1-19

16. Peter, not perfect, but controlled.
John 21:1-19

Used by permission of Mr. Fred Renich

INTRODUCTION

Have you ever stopped to think how insignificant an event it sometimes takes to cause great, far reaching changes? A small book, a little phrase, a brief encounter can change the whole course of a life.

Several years ago someone gave me a handbill with information about a man named Dick Hillis. About Dick Hillis it said, "Prisoner of the Communists in China for two years." But it also mentioned a Ray Stedman, Pastor of Peninsula Bible Church in California, and because I had never met a Californian, I went to hear him. The message was good, and just to see what a Californian was like, I went afterward to meet him. He was sun-tanned, chubby, and nice. And out of that simple encounter with two men, the whole course of my life was changed. Through Ray Stedman and Dr. Dick Hillis, God got me out of

Argentina and directed me into Overseas Crusades. That contact opened doors to the ministry of evangelism that God has given us. If I had not met Ray, I would probably still be in Argentina ministering in a little assembly as if there were no other saints or sinners in the world.

A similar thing could happen to you. You may be feeling uptight and limited in your experiences. You may feel like you are being crowded and hemmed in by life. I believe the Holy Spirit is waiting to open doors that you have never dreamed of. He is waiting to turn your life around with a word, an encounter, a seemingly insignificant event. There is a little phrase I like that ought to be in the Bible. It says, "Big doors turn on small hinges." A little meeting, a short talk could open up your whole future. Further counsel is available by writing to Luis Palau, P.O. Box 1173, Portland, Oregon 97207.

Chapter 1

SIMON, MEET PETER!

When I was a young man, no one taught me how to live the victorious Christian life. I sincerely wanted to be victorious. The only thing I knew how to do was put up a smoke screen, to wear a mask. When I asked other Christians about it, all they could tell me was to read the Bible more, pray more, and witness more. But those things did not change me. "How long is this thing going to go on?" I asked. "When am I going to arrive?"

It took me about eight years to learn the lesson that it is not what you are doing for God, but rather what He wants to do in you and through you that counts. (See Gal. 2:20.)

When Peter met Jesus Christ, he did not realize what the future held for him. He was just a laborer,

1

a poor man who earned his living fishing every night. He spent his days going out on his boat and mending his nets, until the day he encountered Jesus Christ. He didn't know who Jesus was. His brother Andrew picked him up and brought him to Jesus, and the moment he met the Christ, Simon the fisherman began a new life. The incident is recorded in John 1:40-43, and is a very interesting encounter.

"One of the two men who had heard what John said and had followed Jesus was Andrew, Simon Peter's brother. He went straight off and found his own brother, Simon, and told him, 'We have found the Messiah!' (meaning, of course, Christ). And he brought him to Jesus.

"Jesus looked steadily at him and said: 'You are Simon, the son of John. From now on your name is Cephas' (that is, Peter, meaning 'a rock')."

Simon had never met the Lord Jesus. Yet the moment he came face to face with Him, the Lord not only told him his name, but He changed his name and made him a fantastic promise. Jesus told him, "By the time I'm through with you, Simon son of John, people are not going to call you Simon any more. Instead they are going to call you Peter, the rock."

What God is going to do in Peter's life serves as an excellent example of how God works His will. Through Peter we can watch God's redemption, His salvation work itself out.

Redemption is characterized by three stages. First, there is redemption past. Secondly, redemption present. Finally, there is redemption future.

Redemption Past

Redemption past has been settled at the cross forever. Past redemption had to do with guilt and forgiveness of sins. When Christ died on the cross, He finished the work of redemption. The Bible says, "We have redemption through his blood, the forgiveness of [our] sins" (Eph. 1:7, *KJV*). That redemption, that forgiveness is final and is freely available to everyone who accepts Christ. Redemption past guarantees that as a man or woman, boy or girl, your sins are forgiven and all washed away. It guarantees that everything in your past, all the nitty-gritty, all the hanky-panky, all that is condemning is forgiven and washed away through the blood of Christ on the cross. It is a great feeling to begin life anew after salvation. That is redemption past and it is available through the blood at the cross. I hope all of you have experienced that forgiveness—that redemption.

Redemption Future

Redemption future will occur when the Lord gives us a total experience of Himself. He is going to take us out of this place of sin, this world, and make us perfect forever. And when we are perfect, there will be no more problems, no more suffering, no more rebellion, no more temptations, no more anything that drags us down and tends to destroy us. There will be no more sin! Future redemption will be final redemption.

Redemption Now

Redemption now is the stage which concerns all believers. How God works out redemption now is what we will see in the life of Peter. The things which happened to Peter can teach us valuable principles about how God works. We can apply Peter's experience of God to the life of a young man of 17 or 18, or to a young woman questioning God's will for her future, or a woman of 70 who feels, perhaps, that she can no longer serve God at her age. What does God want from our lives? He wants to change us from self-centered men and women into mature, spirit-controlled vessels so that we will be free from the tyranny of selfishness which tends to make us ego-centered, proud, haughty people whom God cannot use to work His will.

In the life of Peter, each one of us is going to see himself. Even young boys and girls who get to know Peter will find that Peter is just like everyone of us. He possesses all the faults and frailties we wish did not exist in ourselves. For that reason, a study of Peter might be very uncomfortable for some—and perhaps a bit frightening. But the rewards of watching God work are so thrilling that Peter's life becomes a great blessing to those who watch and learn.

THE FIRST STEP
God Works Out Redemption Now

There are two things to notice about Peter's initial

encounter with Jesus. First, notice that the Lord looked at Peter as the old man, unredeemed, and *He called him by his old name, Simon.* Now, Simon Peter was an interesting character. He was an aggressive, boastful, self-confident, loud-mouthed and impulsive man. Just imagine him when his brother brought him to Jesus. Peter came, possibly, with a swagger and a cynical look, thinking, "who in the world can this man be to cause my brother to be so interested in introducing me?"

The Lord Jesus looked at him and, of course, knew all that he was thinking. Imagine what a sobering experience it must have been for a man like Peter to have Jesus so quickly and simply tell him who he was. Jesus said, "You are Simon, the son of John." With that, Jesus cut through all the details of his life, all the qualities that made up the character of Peter and, with a name described the natural man, the old man. Christ was saying vastly more to Peter than it might seem on the surface. He was saying, "Simon, I know you. You are yet unrepentant and unredeemed, but before I'm through with you, you will have come all the way to Me flat on your face in humility. I will teach you to know yourself as I know you. And I will change your name to Peter, the rock, because you are crucial to My work."

There is a great deal of Simon in every believer. All of us are, at best, sincere hypocrites. Contradictory as it sounds, it is possible to be a sincere hypocrite. Most people believe that hypocrisy is the worst possible vice for a Christian to have, but many of those same people are sincere hypocrites. If the truth were

5

known, each of us at one time or another has been a sincere hypocrite.

Sincere Hypocrite

When I was a young Christian I sincerely wanted to be rid of obstacles to growth. But I didn't know how to do it. So after a few months of trying and failing, I became a marvelous actor. I knew it was a big put on. But you know, it was a sincere put on. Christians were supposed to be happy, and since I wanted desperately to be a good Christian I pretended great joy, even when I was miserable. Perhaps I thought that if I pretended hard enough the pretense would come true. Unfortunately, it doesn't work that way.

I became so good an actor that I can remember mothers coming to me and saying, "Oh, Louie, if only my son Charlie were just like you. I would be so thrilled if he were as dedicated and as holy as you are." I'd respond with, "Madam, if you only knew my heart, you wouldn't want Charlie to be like me." And Charlie's mother would say, "Oh, and you're so humble on top of it all!"

I had managed, in my great effort to be a sincere Christian, to impress others to such a degree that they believed my charade. They thought I was something which inside I knew I wasn't.

Like so many thousands, Peter didn't know the secret of a happy life, but he sure made a good impression because of his smoke screen of self-con-

6

fidence. As we pursue our study of Peter, we will discover that Peter was in many ways the most impressive of all the disciples, and yet he was one who needed to learn the most dramatic lessons.

Future Promise

"So, you are Simon, the son of John," said Jesus, knowing every detail of Peter's life and thoughts. But Jesus didn't stop with a description of the natural man. A second thing happened when Peter encountered Jesus. Jesus went on to say, *"You shall be called Peter, the rock."* Jesus could look at Peter and say to him, "Simon, listen to Me. I know all the skeletons in your closet, every one of them. If I were to open you up and let people see inside, you would run away in fear and mortification. But, Simon, I love you. And because I love you, I'm going to take hold of you, and by the time I'm through with you, I'm going to redeem you, I'm going to control you. I'm going to mold you so much that your character and your life are going to be different. You will be so altered by the time I'm through with you, Simon, that we'll have to change your name. You will be called Peter because you will be a rock to help other people."

With the dynamic of Christ behind that promise, Peter didn't stand a chance. It happened. What Jesus promises, happens. And if it happened to Simon, it can happen to anyone open to Christ. Simon had all the weaknesses, all the sins that you and I struggle with. Yet by the time Jesus Christ was

7

through He made Simon the great apostle Peter.

This is the basis of our hope. Jesus promises, "You shall be. . . ." The Lord didn't say, "Maybe, Simon. Perhaps, if you're good, Simon." He said, "You *shall* be a rock." Philippians 1:6 says, "I feel sure that the one who has begun his good work in you will go on developing it until the day of Jesus Christ." When God takes a man in hand, no matter how wild a character he may be, He changes him. God makes him what he ought to be.

When Jesus changed Simon's name, He was looking several years ahead. Peter was at that time a long way from being a rock, but Jesus knew there would come a time when Peter and only a handful of others would turn the world upside down with their faith and power.

Maturation Process

First Thessalonians 5:24 promises, "He who calls you is utterly faithful and he will finish what he has set out to do." He will do it. You may say to yourself, "If you knew me, you wouldn't be so positive. Nobody can handle me. I have such rotten passions, such a twisted mind that I can't straighten myself out." And you would be right. You can't do it. That's true. But if you will let Jesus Christ who indwells you take over, He will do it for you. Jesus has given His word.

Peter had gone through many of these same experiences. He was up one day and down the next. We can watch his progress and his decay and then his strong progress again as he really begins to grow up.

All of us when we receive Jesus Christ are just spiritual babies. But once Christ begins His work in us, we begin to grow from babyhood into spiritual adolescence, and then into maturity in Jesus Christ because Christ is at work in our hearts.

Have you heard the voice of Jesus Christ as Peter did? What has God said to you by way of fact and promise? He knows you as He knew Peter and He can change you as He did Peter. Has He said, "I want to do something with you"?

God changes young men and women; God changes adult men and women. Perhaps God has promised you a change through the Scriptures, or through the Holy Spirit. If God has spoken to you, then you can expect Him to do what He has promised to do. You can expect Him to turn you around and change your name.

Chapter 2

START WALKING ON WATER

God is still at work in the world today, and many interesting things are happening. God, to do His work, utilizes men and women. He does not operate indirectly. Very seldom He go to a man without the intervention of another human being.

Some people would like to boast and say, "Nobody ever evangelized me. I got it straight from heaven." When asked how this revelation occurred they may respond, "Well, I was reading the Bible." Such persons forget that God used His Holy Spirit to convey the Word, and somebody translated that Word, and somebody printed it. Somebody donated the money to publish it. So, don't glory in yourself, rather give the glory to God.

The Lord loves to work through people. But He can only work through a special kind of people.

11

People like Simon Peter, and people like you and me who are willing to be changed can be used by God to do amazing things. But, before He can really work through us, He has to begin to polish us and mature us and make us grow. He can use us from the beginning, but if He is really to use a man He must work him over. All of us carry around much excess baggage that needs to go. We have many attitudes, habits, weights, and so many ways about us that are undesirable that He simply has to make changes before He can use us.

We saw in Peter a beginning of a process of maturing. In the first encounter with Jesus Christ in John 1:42, we saw two little things, but they marked a crucial beginning. First, a fact. Jesus Christ looked Simon over and said, "Simon, you are the son of John." By saying that, Jesus was saying a great deal. He was saying, "Simon, I know you. You cannot fool Me. You may fool others. You may fool your fellow fishermen. You may deceive the businessmen with whom you're in the fishing industry, but I know you. You are Simon. I know all about you."

Second, Jesus Christ didn't just catalog the skeletons in his closet. After letting Simon know he was exposed for what he was, Jesus gave him a promise. That was the basis for Peter's hope. That is the basis for our hope.

We all start life in a very carnal way. All of us, when we are born, are very self-centered individuals. Even the nicest baby is selfish and very, very egotistical. The sad thing about this is that many people go all through life entirely self-centered. And even many Christians after they receive Christ, unless they allow the indwelling Christ to pick them up and raise them to maturity, are forever spiritual babies. You and I both know thousands of Christians who are spiritual babies. Humanly speaking, they may be 40, 50, 60 years old, but spiritually speaking, they continue to act and behave very immaturely. In church, at home, in relations with their wives, they still have temper tantrums, they still throw things around, and they still hit doors. They are still acting like babies on the spiritual plane.

We can look at Peter's life and see how God worked at picking him up and taking him from Spiritual immaturity to Spiritual maturity. We find Peter encountering Jesus Christ as a spiritual baby and then experiencing Him as a growing believer, and finally conducting himself as a Spirit-filled apostle. Peter stumbled and faltered along the way as all growing Christians will, but by God's grace he recovered and continued his walk to perfect maturity.

THE SECOND STEP
God Controls Circumstances of Life

The Lord Jesus Christ did not leave Simon alone after his introduction and name change. Christ began to take Peter and lead him step by step towards maturity. Peter's introduction to Christ was only the first step. In Luke 5:4-11, we find the second step which we will call providence, or circumstances of life controlled by God.

"When [Jesus] had finished speaking, he said to Simon, 'Push out now into deep water and let down your nets for a catch.'

"Simon replied, 'Master! We've worked all night and never caught a thing, but if you say so I'll let the nets down.'

"And when they had done this, they caught an enormous shoal of fish—so big that the nets began to tear. So they signaled to their friends in the other boat to come and help them. They came and filled both the boats to sinking point. When Simon Peter saw this, he fell on his knees before Jesus and said, 'Keep away from me, Lord, for I'm only a sinful man!'

"For he and his companions [including Zebedee's sons, James and John, Simon's partners] were staggered at the haul of fish that they had made.

"Jesus said to Simon: 'Don't be afraid, Simon. From now on your catch will be men.'

"So they brought the boats ashore, left everything and followed him."

Not long ago I talked with a man twenty years old who was a college student. He told me a familiar story. "The thing that bothers me," he confessed, "is that I've received Christ as my Saviour, but I have all the same problems I had before. I don't have victory. When I ask Christians what the solution is I'm told to read the Bible more, pray more, and witness more. I've been doing that faithfully and haven't yet found the secret of real victory. It seems all I do is struggle, struggle, struggle, and it isn't a pleasant experience. Jesus Christ is my Saviour, but

14

I don't feel He's real to me. I want to feel that He's alive to me, that He's right here controlling and directing me as I try to walk with God."

This was also Peter's experience until Christ intervened. God often has to send into our lives some dramatic experience to wake us up and make us face the fact that Jesus Christ can be a reality in our lives. Our first encounter with Christ is often only the introduction.

Brokenness of Heart

In Peter's second meeting with Christ we can begin to see an example of that providence which illustrates that God is at work in the circumstances of a Christian's life. Two things happened to Peter here. First, *Peter saw something of his own heart.* When the great catch of fish had taken place, Simon fell at the feet of Jesus and said, "Keep away from me, Lord, for I'm only a sinful man!" (Luke 5:8). Peter realized that he wasn't worthy to meet Jesus as he now saw himself. He had initially doubted when asked to let down his nets, but when the miracle of the fish occurred his honest heart compelled him to fall to his knees in submission.

Each person must individually come to the place where he discovers his own real sinfulness of heart. In this experience Peter faced his. There are many people who are true Christians and have faced their need for salvation and have asked for forgiveness. However, there are many more people who have not.

They refuse to face the wickedness and evil of their own hearts and resent it when told that man is born sinful. They resent evangelists and preachers who dare to call people sinners and evil. A man who hasn't discovered what Peter discovered cannot go very far with God. Until you discover your own wickedness, your own malice, the corruption of your own heart, you can never find God in a living and real way. As long as you continue to believe that you are all right, that you are not all that bad, as long as you think you can make it on your own, you are lost.

I had a conversation once with a 12-year-old boy in Spokane, Washington. After an evangelistic meeting, he asked if I would talk to him. He looked so worried that I wondered what he had on his mind.

He said to me, "Mr. Palau, do you think that God could forgive a rotten sinner?" I looked at him and thought, "Twelve years old. How rotten can a boy be at twelve?"

I asked him to tell me what the rottenness was all about. By the time that boy was through, I was convinced he was rotten. He had experienced much more sin than you can imagine.

I remembered when I was twelve years old. I remembered doing some things in those days that I'd be embarrassed for anyone to find out. This boy was also only twelve; however, he was doing things most of us would never dream of. He was escaping at night to a park with a buddy and engaging in homosexual acts with him. His mom didn't know where he was going or what he was doing. He was convinced that

God could never forgive him and the thought broke his heart.

And that's the place you must come to. No matter how corrupt you have been, when you have a brokenness of heart and you feel God can never forgive you, that is when God can work.

Confirmation of Call

Not only did Peter see something of his own heart in this second meeting with Christ, *he also saw something of what he will be.* In verse 10 Jesus says, "Don't be afraid, Simon. From now on your catch will be men."

The first time the Lord encountered Peter, all He did to him was give him a general overview. "I'm going to deal with you, Peter. You shall be Peter, a rock." The second time, He began to clarify His mission in Peter's life. "Don't be afraid, Peter, from now on you are going to catch men." In other words, He began to specify a little more of what He was prepared to do with Peter's life.

When Christ takes over in a life, He gives us an overview. He promises to forgive and to bless us and make us grow up and become men. Then slowly He begins to point out and clarify what He is going to do with our life. Peter was on his knees, thinking that Christ was going to reject him because he faced his own sinfulness, and instead Christ reconfirmed Peter's call. The first time, Jesus gave Peter a promise. The second time, Jesus gave him a plan.

17

Surrender of Will

There is a third effect on Peter at this encounter. *Peter responded with full surrender of his will.* In verse 11 Peter does a wonderful thing that many young men have done since. "When they had brought their boats to land, they left everything and followed him," (*RSV*).

Now when God calls a man, it does not mean that he necessarily has to sell everything 100 percent and give away the money or put it all in the bank. He may keep his business. We are told in John 21:3 that Peter went back to his boats. How could he have gone back to his trade if he had given them all up three years before? Obedience to God's call does not automatically require material poverty. The important thing, is the full commitment of heart and spirit when Jesus speaks to a man. It is this commitment that Peter had. Somebody else would have to care for the boats and nets in the interval. His business could wait; Jesus Christ could not!

Partnership with God

Three important things have happened to Peter, but there is a fourth thing Peter was about to learn and that is the *fruitfulness of divine partnership*. In Luke 5:5-7, Jesus is recognizing Peter's gifts and acknowledging his abilities. He is saying, in effect, "You're a good fisherman, Peter, but if you and I start working as one, there is no limit to what God can do through your life. There is no limit to the kind of fruitfulness that can take place in your life."

This is a big lesson for any Christian to learn. Most of us are brought up with the idea that when we receive Christ all that remains is to roll up our sleeves and sweat it out for the Lord. Many sincere people commit themselves to serving Christ with all their being. They promise faithfulness, consecration, dedication, devotion, and love. But a few months later they are like a deflated balloon. The Christian commitment that was growing so big and looked so beautiful and full suddenly became flat and limp.

Many who receive Christ and make all these big promises (in some emotional meeting they came forward and consecrated their lives to God), are discouraged and deflated a few months later. Why? Because they have not yet learned what God taught Peter and is trying to teach every man and woman, that we cannot do it alone. John 15:5 says, "I am the vine, you are the branches. He who abides in me, and I in him, he it is that bears much fruit" (*RSV*).

For many of us, it takes years to learn this lesson. We refuse to believe that we can't do it alone. It is especially hard for the man who has a good education, a good Christian background, and knows quite a bit about the Bible. He can't help but believe he can do it alone.

Many people go out in self-confidence and think they can go it alone. They believe that knowing a whole bunch of Scripture verses by memory, finding some good outlines from a Christian magazine, or illustrations from an old book of sermons are all they need to do a job for God. Not many say so openly, of course, but inside most of us who love Christ sincerely think we've got it made. We secretly say, "You're going to see what I can do. Oh, boy, is the Lord going to be proud of this young man. Just let me be."

Controlled by the Holy Spirit

The biggest lesson that the Lord has to teach us is that it is not what we are going to do for God out of self-effort but what Christ, living in us, will do when He is allowed control through the indwelling Holy Spirit.

It took me a very long time to learn this. I received Christ when I was twelve years old. During those first few years I was a typical convert. My counselor was great as a soul winner but a weak spiritual body builder. He was one of those who insisted that just reading, praying, and witnessing would do all that was necessary to make me grow.

It didn't, of course. I cooled off quickly. Then when I was seventeen, the Lord in a marvelous way spoke to my heart, took me out of the foolishness of worldliness and brought me back to Him. I became baptized, and I bought myself a new Bible, and I discovered a strong, new self-confidence. I taught a Sunday School class and held Bible study in my garage. I preached on street corners. I was convinced that if I was dedicated enough, God would use me to do great things.

But during those years from 17 to 25 I had an experience that dragged me down. There was a group of young fellows who worked together in our church. We loved the Lord, but we experienced so many ups and downs that after a while it got tiring. I began to get discouraged and say to myself, "How long is this thing going on? When am I going to finally make it? When do I finally arrive?"

It took me about eight years to learn the lesson that it is not what *you* are doing for God, but rather what *He* wants to do in you and through you that counts. It takes us a long time because we are impatient and arrogant. We don't like the idea that somehow we don't have what it takes. We like to believe that we do. Peter was an excellent example of this misconception.

It was at this point in Peter's life that his salvation became settled. His will was surrendered. First *the Lord called him.* Then *Peter actually became sure of his salvation.* Christ put His hand on him and promised him a life fishing for men. Peter, at this point, left everything and followed the Lord Jesus. He's in. He's made it.

But receiving Christ is only crossing the line. All that Peter had experienced so far was just the beginning. When you receive Christ your sins are forgiven and washed away. Redemption is taken care of. Your past is forgotten and all the skeletons in your closet are buried at the cross. There is no longer anything to worry about in your relationship with God. You've been redeemed.

After salvation comes the business of daily living,

and that is where most of us fail. There are thousands, perhaps millions of evangelicals, true Christians, real children of God, who get stuck right here. And for 30 and 40 years, they never get beyond this point. They're happy that they're saved, they know they're going to heaven, but there's no growth here on earth. Having to function as a Christian, having to operate as a believer every day, having to really live, is where many fail. It's a pitiful sight. But, Peter did *not* stop growing and learning. After the Lord called him, and after Peter actually became sure of his salvation, then Peter took yet a third step.

THE THIRD STEP
God Directs in Obedience of Faith

In Matthew 14:25-31, we read, "In the small hours Jesus went out to them, walking on the water of the lake. When the disciples caught sight of him walking on the water they were terrified. 'It's a ghost!' they said, and screamed with fear.

"But at once Jesus spoke to them, 'It's all right! It's I myself; don't be afraid!'

" 'Lord, if it's really you,' said Peter, 'tell me to come to you on the water.'

" 'Come on, then,' replied Jesus.

"Peter stepped down from the boat and did walk on the water, making for Jesus. But when he saw the fury of the wind he panicked and began to sink, calling out, 'Lord save me!' At once Jesus reached

22

out his hand and caught him, saying, 'You little-faith! What made you lose your nerve like that?' "

The third lesson Peter must learn is *the obedience of faith* to the Word. If we are to continue to grow, we must learn this.

It must have been an exciting way for Peter to take this step. In the middle of high winds and rolling waves, Peter dared to step out of a tossing fishing boat onto the water, believing that the figure coming toward them was his Master. What an outrageous thing to do, and yet the Lord Jesus said, "Come ahead!" What a fantastic moment that must have been! Few Christians get to test their obedience and faith in such dramatic ways. The sad thing is that too few Christians dare or bother to test their faith in any way at all.

Test of Faith

It seems that God made us to expect life to be exciting. We are always looking for excitement. We are looking for joy, for happiness. Some people try to suppress these feelings. They believe that the Christian life is not supposed to be joyful and they are afraid of appearing to enjoy themselves too much, or of finding life too exciting. This strange impression is certainly not supported by Scripture. What could possibly be more exciting than walking on water?

I remember in my church in Argentina preachers used to spend whole sermons trying to distinguish between "joy" and "happiness." I never understood that. They taught that it was one thing to be joyful, but that is not happiness. "Happiness is very superficial," they would say, "but joy is very deep." I can't believe that a person can be happy and feel excitement and not be joyful, nor be joyful and not happy. If a person is joyful, he is going to be happy, and if not he doesn't know what happiness really is. We thrive on these dramatic feelings.

Peter was looking for excitement when he said, "Lord let me come." And the Lord said, "Come ahead, I have a lesson to teach you." The Lord delights in teaching lessons to His children.

Isn't it great to know that He loves us in spite of our conceit and arrogance? And that He can teach us humility, faith and trust. Yet He is gracious and does it in a loving way. He doesn't push us too much, although He sometimes lets us corner ourselves. When that happens, all we need to do is call, "Lord help me!" and He will immediately reach out His hand and catch us.

When Peter obeyed Jesus Christ's call to walk on the water, Peter walked on the water. Peter put his faith into action and obeyed. Obedience is faith in action.

Many people who claim that they follow Jesus Christ and do extreme things in their own strength actually dishonor Jesus Christ. A fanatic walks on his own steam. Eventually his pretense will fail him and he will begin to struggle and sink. Peter, however, walked on God's command. There is a vast difference between the two.

Walk on Water

One of the biggest lessons that God wants to teach us is how to start walking on water. Start stepping out by faith. Dare to step out on whatever God has said to you as a family, or as an individual. There may be some person to whom God spoke ten years ago and has been speaking to ever since with no response. If God has been faithful in reminding you that He spoke to you sometime, somewhere about something, find the courage to step out by faith on the Word of Jesus Christ. Lack of courage results in a dull, barren, and unfruitful life; a life of discouragement as a Christian. And, chances are, all the time in the back of your mind the Holy Spirit keeps nagging, pleading with you to obey the Word of God that He spoke to you so many years ago. If you could dare to step out you would enjoy the fulness of the Holy Spirit and begin to walk in the fulness of the Spirit. It is not too late to respond to Him.

Every Christian ought to learn to walk on water. All through the Bible, God's chosen are called "men of faith." What does that mean? Basically it means acting with the courage Peter displayed.

Abraham was one of these great men of faith. He didn't walk on water, but he walked on desert sand at God's command. Hebrews 11:8 tells us, "It was by faith that Abraham obeyed the summons to go out to a place which he would eventually possess, and he set out in complete ignorance of his destination." When God called Abraham, he had no idea where God was taking him. Imagine the faith it took

[handwritten margin note: What has he said!?]

to believe God and step out. All he had was God's statement, "Abraham, I'm going to give you a land for your descendants. And they will number more than the stars in the sky or grains of sand on the shore. Come with me and I will take you to this land." It was enough for Abraham to know that it was God who spoke, and he began moving by faith in the will of God. Abraham's obedience was faith in action.

Any believer can have the same experience of God when he begins to walk by faith in the indwelling Holy Spirit. Once Peter, or any Christian, obeys the Lord and steps out, he will be able to do anything, because all things are possible to one who believes.

Impossible as it seemed, Peter believed he would walk to Jesus on the water and stepped out on faith toward Christ. When Peter got near Jesus, he suddenly took his eyes off Him and immediately began to sink. But when he cried, "Lord help me!" Jesus stretched out His hand, picked him up and said, "Why did you doubt, man of small faith?"

It is entirely possible, human nature being what it is, that at the moment Peter stood on the heaving water, looked back at the men in the boat, and considered that very few people had ever stood on water, he exclaimed, "Hey, look at me. I'm standing on water!" Christ had been forgotten and Peter was exalting in his feat.

Power from God

So many of us forget where the power in our lives

comes from. We have a spiritual experience, an answer to prayer, or we win a soul to Jesus Christ and at that moment of glory and excitement, we suddenly forget that it was the power of God at work through our life. The moment we become self-confident, down we go.

It must have hurt Peter when the Lord asked him where his faith had gone. After all, he *had* stepped out of the boat onto the waves. He *had* walked on water all the way to Christ. And yet Christ told him he was lacking in faith. God *expects* us to obey so He can show us His power, and we are often surprised by how great it is. Little things for God seem so momentous to us.

I remember the first time that God answered one of my prayers. It was such a simple request that I almost hesitate to tell about it.

While we were living in Argentina I read the story of George Mueller, a great man of faith. I was working in a bank at the time which had been on strike for forty-two days. You can imagine what a mess the banking system was at that time. They paid no salaries during this period. My mother was a widow. I had five sisters and one young brother. We had absolutely run out of money. After reading this book about the experiences of George Mueller I said, "Lord, I have never actually experienced for myself a true answer to prayer. I wish that You would show me one answer to prayer. Send me some money for the bus to go to the bank. Send it to me in some way that indicates that it came from You." I'd seen many answers to my mother's prayers. I knew she had faith and I knew that the Lord answered prayer, but I wanted an answer for me.

That morning I got up early since the bank opened at 7:00 in the summer. In my mind, I figured that the way the Lord would answer my request would be to have someone drop a quarter for me to find which would pay my way to the bank. To show how little faith one has even when expecting God to work, I got up in plenty of time to walk to the bank if I had to in case the money didn't come. When I left the house it was dark. All the way to the bus stop I searched for the quarter that I knew would be there. I got to the corner and looked around. I examined people fumbling for their change. I looked everywhere but found no quarter. Maybe the Lord's quarter was not at this bus stop, and since there was another bus stop several blocks away, I walked to that one. When I arrived I looked and looked. No quarter. There was one more bus line that went into town about eight blocks farther on. The quarter just had to be at that one.

I had walked about three blocks in the fog and dark when I heard someone trying to push a car out of a garage. He was huffing and puffing but couldn't push it out. I offered him some help and between the two of us we pushed the car out of the garage. As it rolled down a little hill, it started up and off he disappeared into the fog. I continued on my way the three blocks to the final bus stop still without a quarter. Then, suddenly in the fog, I heard a car idling. It was the fellow that I had helped. He opened the window and apologized for not offering me a ride and asked where I was going. When I told him, he said he worked at the bank across the street and would be happy to give me a ride.

It may not sound earth-shattering to you, but my answer to prayer was very exciting to me. It was only worth a quarter, but to me it was a tremendous test. It was my first experience with God getting through my doubts and answering prayer.

Little Faith to Big Faith

When we conducted a crusade in Lima, Peru, we wanted to televise it. The team member directing the crusade wrote, "Luis, we've got to have money to nail down the contract." I wrote back, "Sign the contract. We don't have any money, but I believe the Lord's going to send it."

We were actually $500 in the red in our mission account. I had faith as we prayed at home, that God was going to send the money. They signed the contract. The crusade began—the first night, second night, third night—and we still didn't have the $2,500 we needed. The manager had no idea we didn't have a cent to pay for the program.

On the fourth day a cable came from Pat, my wife, which said, "Praise the Lord. Longhill Chapel in Chatham, New Jersey, has sent in $2,500 for television." The church didn't even know we needed it.

There were several years between the first quarter and the $2,500. It took practice and experience in faith to receive this delightful reward. But you have to begin.

The exciting thing about beginning to practice walking by faith is that God delights in giving us these experiences. Maybe we sometimes ask silly things. What right did Peter have to expect to walk on water? Yet the Lord told him to come ahead and experience the reward for his faith.

Step out and begin to walk on water. No matter what area of your life you've been wondering about, believe that the Lord will give you the excitement and the blessing of answering your little faith. But your little faith is going to be very exciting to you. Little faith becomes big faith when we begin to practice it day after day.

Chapter 3

WHAT NOW, LORD?

It is heartbreaking to have a baby that never grows up. We love little babies but we expect them to grow. Many Christians, unfortunately, remain at the infant level of immaturity long after they should be showing signs of growth. In our study of the life of Peter, we all have seen a little of ourselves. We all must experience the first encounter with Jesus Christ. Then we are shown ourselves as we really are. If we are responsive as Peter was, we fall on our knees and confess our sinfulness and Christ gives us His forgiveness. If we continue in our growth and obedience in Christ, He shows us His power and helps us walk on water. Peter learned these first lessons well. The greater tests were yet to come.

THE FOURTH STEP
God Claims Complete Authority

John 6:48-69 records the turning point in Peter's life. Jesus Christ is speaking. " 'I myself am the bread of life. Your forefathers ate manna in the desert, and they died. This is bread that comes down from Heaven, so that a man may eat it and not die. I myself am the living bread which came down from Heaven, and if anyone eats this bread he will live for ever. The bread which I will give is my body and I shall give it for the life of the world.'

"This led to a fierce argument among the Jews, some of them saying, 'How can this man give us his body to eat?'

"So Jesus said to them: 'Unless you do eat the body of the Son of Man and drink his blood, you are not really living at all. The man who eats my flesh and drinks my blood has eternal life and I will raise him up when the last day comes. For my body is real food and my blood is real drink. The man who eats my body and drinks my blood shares my life and I share his. Just as the living Father sent me and I am alive because of the Father, so the man who lives on me will live because of me. This is the bread which came down from Heaven! It is not like the manna which your forefathers used to eat, and died. The man who eats this bread will live forever.'

"Jesus said all these things while teaching in the synagogue at Capernaum. Many of his disciples heard him say these things, and commented, 'This is hard teaching indeed; who could accept that?'

"Then Jesus, knowing intuitively that his disciples were complaining about what he had just said, went on: 'Is this too much for you? Then what would happen if you were to see the Son of Man going up to the place where he was before? It is the Spirit which gives life. The flesh will not help you. The things which I have told you are spiritual and are life. But some of you will not believe me.'

"For Jesus knew from the beginning which of his followers did not trust him and who was the man who would betray him. Then he added, 'This is why I said to you, "No one can come to me unless my Father puts it into his heart to come."'

"As a consequence of this, many of his disciples withdrew and no longer followed him. So Jesus said to the twelve, 'And are you too wanting to go away?'

"'Lord,' answered Simon Peter, 'who else should we go to? Your words have the ring of eternal life! And we believe and are convinced that you are the holy one of God.'

"Jesus replied, 'Did I not choose you twelve—and one of you has the devil in his heart?'

"He was speaking of Judas, the son of Simon Iscariot, one of the twelve, who was planning to betray him."

Sifting and Testing

Everyone has to come to terms with the Bible—not just as a book, but as a living message, a living word from God. A person cannot really know Jesus Christ unless he accepts the Word of God in its fulness. Then he can begin to enjoy the Christian life. Learning to obey the Word of God can be a perplexing process. Scripture divides and tests all those who come in contact with it.

Christ often used very controversial teachings to shake people up. It sometimes seems that He deliberately intended to shock people. In the above passage He was talking to the Jews. Many people were following Him. They had seen His miracles. They had been fed by the bread that He had multiplied. It was quite exciting to follow a miracle worker, and Jesus had acquired quite a following. But Jesus, after He had done those miracles and showed some of the excitement of walking with Him, began to really sift through and test His admirers. He used some very hard language and difficult concepts in speaking to them. For instance, He says, "If you want to have eternal life, you've got to eat my flesh and drink my blood." This was a shocking statement to say to His followers. The first ones to drop out were the people who were unbelievers. They didn't want to have a thing to do with Him, and His controversial teachings gave them good reason to conclude that this man was out of His mind.

But it wasn't just the unbelieving Jews who dropped out. Many of those who had begun to call themselves disciples of Jesus were troubled. In verse 60 we're told, "Many of his disciples heard him say these things, and commented, 'This is hard teaching indeed; who could accept that?' " The Lord Jesus knew exactly what He was doing; He was testing to find out if

34

they really believed that He had the answers.

Every one of us, even those brought up in a Christian atmosphere, has to confront this question. Does Jesus Christ have the answer? Many face this issue when they go to a secular college and meet self-sufficient, unbelieving professors who refute the Bible and question Christianity and our parents' beliefs. The student brought up in a Christian home suddenly has to make a decision for himself. Who has the answers for us? Is it Jesus Christ or is it this educated, self-sufficient professor who has the audacity to doubt Jesus Christ, question the Bible, and make fun of Christianity? It's a traumatic experience that we all have to face, but an essential one. Because until we determine who our authority is we really are a long way from maturity. Until we accept the authority of Jesus Christ over our rational processes, we are still floundering babies.

After talking about the blood and losing many followers, we might expect Jesus to drop the issue, but He wasn't finished. Some of the disciples had dropped out, so He called the intimate group, the Twelve, and asked them if they wished to leave also. You see, the issue was not the precise wording of the doctrine about eating His body and drinking His blood. The issue was, are you going to follow Jesus Christ all the way even when what He says offends your sensibilities? Are you willing to follow Him even if He sounds irrational?

When Jesus asked that question, Peter said, "Lord, who else should we go to? Your words have the ring of eternal life!" (v. 68). With those words, Peter settled

35

for himself the question of who has the answers.

Accepting the Right Authority

We have to come to the place where we forget what the professor has to say, what the psychologist has to say, and what the historian has to say when it conflicts with Christ's words. As Christians we must accept the Bible in its entirety as the inspired Word of God, believe it, and love it.

This doesn't imply an irrational acceptance without thought and intelligent question. It does mean that you accept His authority and the authority of the Word of God in the face of unbelieving attack on its principles. Thousands of Christians will actually function on the basis of what some secularist says and ignore what the Word of God says. Many sincere but avoidable mistakes are made this way.

I read an article recently in which a psychiatrist from Chicago seemed to suggest to rising young executives that if their wives stand in the way of professional success they should get rid of them. Therefore, if you want to become a success in a big company and your wife endangers your chances because she happens to be overweight or for some other reason doesn't create a good impression, this authority suggests you get rid of her. Here is a man with three doctorates from the best universities and because he speaks with education and authority, many Christians may be influenced, and before they know it, some of them are uncritically accepting what such men say.

Then they are surprised when they become dissatisfied in the home.

Christians have to decide who they are going to follow. If you still doubt the word of Jesus Christ and His authority, don't be surprised if you keep floundering and vacillating back and forth reading the pseudo-intellectuals who deny the existence of God, who deny the reality of Jesus Christ, and then dare to tell us how to live and how to make family decisions. Anyone who denies these basic truths is not an authority for you and me.

Peter settled the issue for himself when he decided to stay with Christ and His teachings. Paul, in 2 Timothy 3:16 states, "All scripture is inspired by God and is useful for teaching the faith and correcting error, for resetting the direction of a man's life and training him in good living."

Once you have settled Christ's authority over you, and have given Him the supremacy in your life, then you can listen to the others without being shaken. You can read what they have to say and weigh it intelligently and critically because everything they say is judged in the light of Scripture. When you can do this you will be a real intellectual, not a pseudo-intellectual. Anyone who denies the existence of God and authority of the Word is a pseudo-intellectual because he has neglected the most critical learning a man can obtain. So many of the people that we pay attention to in the mass media are defeated men in their personal lives because the most important dimension of reality is neglected—the spiritual truths of Scripture.

37

When you settle the authority of Jesus Christ, you are free to be a real intellectual. A college student who settles the authority of Christ and of the Word of God can go to any class and is not going to be shaken by any professor. Because he knows God personally, and because he has settled the issue of authority in his life, everything the professor says, can be judged by that standard. Such a student can comfortably listen. He can comfortably accept statements which are consistent with eternal truths, and he doesn't have to accept those which are not. His faith cannot be shattered or shaken. He can look opposition in the face and actually enjoy a good debate, because there is no problem, no threat. His authority is settled. Jesus Christ is the last word for him.

The growing believer constantly undergoes testing of his faith in God's authority. There is a constant sifting in a believer's life. Can you accept the hard things of the Lord as well as the sweet rewards and blessings? That is a good measuring rod of maturity. Scripture records many hard things which God commanded that are serious stumbling blocks to some believers. They just can't accept God asking the people of Israel to wipe out a whole tribe—men, women, even children and animals. There are very good explanations for God commanding such things. When you have the audacity to question the wisdom of God, you are suggesting that you are more morally enlightened than God Himself.

Jesus Christ tested Peter at this point. If you think that you are very mature and spiritual when you question the hard things of the Lord, you are mistaken. Actually, you are showing your spiritual babyhood. You are showing that you haven't developed enough. You are also showing that you haven't studied Scripture enough because challenging God's authority is a manifestation of a lack of study.

God never makes mistakes, so, when we challenge His hard sayings, we are really challenging His authority. We have not settled the issue of authority if we still want to keep the right to pick and choose what we like from the Scriptures. The sooner we accept His Word by faith, the sooner we'll be delivered from the kind of chastisement and discipline that Peter had to go through. Even after his commitment to stay with Christ, Peter was still challenging His authority in his heart. He had much to learn yet.

THE FIFTH STEP
God Reveals Christ as His Son

Matthew 16:13-20 says, "When Jesus reached the Caesarea-Philippi district he asked his disciples a question. 'Who do people say the Son of Man is?'

" 'Well, some say John the Baptist,' they told him. 'Some say Elijah, others Jeremiah or one of the prophets.'

" 'But what about you?' he said to them. 'Who do you say that I am?'

"Simon Peter answered, 'You? You are Christ, the Son of the living God!'

" 'Simon, son of Jonah, you are a fortunate man

indeed!' said Jesus, 'for it was not your own nature but my Heavenly Father who has revealed this truth to you! Now I tell you that you are Peter the rock, and it is on this rock that I am going to found my Church, and the powers of death will never prevail against it. I will give you the keys of the kingdom of Heaven; whatever you forbid on earth will be what is forbidden in Heaven and whatever you permit on earth will be what is permitted in Heaven!' Then he impressed on his disciples that they should not tell anyone that he was Christ."

Scripture here gives us the *revelation of Christ as God.* How excited Jesus must have felt to realize that these men had finally begun to understand who He was. And when Christ asked His men who they thought He was, Peter gave Him the answer He was looking for. "You are Christ, the Son of the living God!" This is the answer that the world is waiting to hear.

Measure of Maturity

The revelation of Jesus Christ as God has to come to the heart *by the Holy Spirit.* One cannot argue this revelation into a person. One can only quote the verses and make a theological appeal. But until the Holy Spirit takes this truth and reveals it to the heart, man finds it difficult to believe. It is a work of the Spirit.

The Lord Jesus said in Matthew 11:25, "O Father, Lord of Heaven and earth, I thank you for hiding these things from the clever and intelligent and for showing them to mere children." There has to be a humility of the heart before Christ can reveal Himself as the Son of God to us.

Jesus was undoubtedly thrilled at Peter's confession and blessed him for it. "Simon, son of Jonah, you are a fortunate man indeed! For it was not your own nature but my Heavenly Father who has revealed this truth to you! Now I tell you . . ." and He follows His blessing by making some promises to Peter.

Accepting Christ isn't a question of saying, "Well, I kind of like Him. My mother believed in Him. When I was young we used to get on our knees beside our bed and pray to Jesus. It felt good, but I don't know if He's the Son of God."

If that is where you stand, you are in bad shape. Either Jesus Christ is who He said He was, or He is the biggest deceiver that ever lived. He claimed to be God, the Son, revealed in the flesh. Salvation cannot occur until a sinner comes to that place where he wholly accepts that Jesus Christ is the anointed one, the Christ, the Son of the living God. The greatest moment in the life of Peter came when he said, "You are the Christ, Son of the living God."

With this realization, Peter stepped into a greater measure of maturity. And at that, the Lord Jesus confirmed His promise to Peter. He said, in effect, "Now you indeed *are* Peter. Now you *are* the rock. Your confession confirms that you are standing on solid ground."

Spiritual maturity begins for the believer when the full impact of who Christ is becomes real. It begins when a man suddenly understands that this living Christ who dwells within him is the Son of the living God. Not just a Saviour. Not just a great Saviour, but the Son of the living God dwelling within him.

This is the realization that changed my spiritual life—that the living Christ lived within Luis Palau. I tell you, that was the beginning of a new, real life for me.

The Bible teaches that when a man is joined to the Lord he becomes one spirit with Him. Suddenly it is not I going through life on my own with a little wisdom from the outside. It is I, indwelled and controlled by the Son of God. Such a miracle cannot help but change a man's life.

Commission of Authority

Peter is blessed by Christ and *is made a promise*. The commission Christ gave to Peter is made clear and explained. The commission is recorded in Matthew 16:18, "You are Peter the rock, and it is on this rock that I am going to found my Church, and the powers of death will never prevail against it. I will give you the keys of the kingdom of Heaven; whatever you forbid on earth will be what is forbidden in Heaven and whatever you permit on earth will be what is permitted in Heaven."

Matthew 18:17-20 says, "And if he still won't pay any attention, tell the matter to the church. And if he won't even listen to the church then he must be to you just like a pagan—or a tax collector!

"Believe me, whatever you forbid upon earth will be what is forbidden in Heaven, and whatever you permit on earth will be what is permitted in Heaven.

"And I tell you once more that if two of you on earth agree in asking for anything it will be granted to you by my Heavenly Father. For wherever two or three people come together in my name, I am there, right among them!"

Notice the tremendous authority that Christ gave to Peter. On the faith that Peter represented, Christ would build His church. The real Church, the body of Christ, is built on people who believe that Jesus Christ is God the Son. The deity of Christ is the rock, and all who believe can lay claim to the authority Christ gave Peter after his confession. We can claim that authority because Jesus is God and dwells within us.

What did Jesus mean by the keys of the Kingdom of Heaven? The keys are an expression, an example of the fact that our authority in Christ is not limited to earth. Whatever we permit on earth is permitted in heaven, whatever we bind here is bound there. That is authority! I see three implications in the keys—*privilege, authority* and *responsibility*.

Think of the *privilege* of having the keys to the Kingdom of God. When you take a Bible and witness to someone in the name of Jesus Christ, you are exercising the privileges of the keys of the kingdom. You can speak with *authority*. You don't have to be apologetic or unsure. You can say, with boldness, that Jesus Christ is the Son of God and that He changes lives and gives peace with God.

A newsman who had met Billy Graham many times wrote these words: "The thing that shakes me up about Billy Graham is his arrogant humility." What an interesting description. That is what our authority in Christ permits each one of us to have—arrogant humility.

In addition to privilege and authority, the keys suggest *responsibility*. Some of us would rather pass responsibility on to ministers and teachers. We would rather be little anonymous nobodys. When you have the indwelling Christ, you are growing in Him. The Bible has authority over your life. You have the right, His authority, to speak in the name of the Lord Jesus Christ. But more, you have the responsibility.

For me, this responsibility is an exciting thing in our crusade evangelism because it is such a blessing to move into a city, and in the name of Jesus Christ claim that city for God. Because we've come in the name of Jesus Christ and we have the keys to the kingdom, we have the privilege, the responsibility, and the authority to move in as representatives of Him. The same is true for any man in his business, in his office, or in his executive suite. He is there, not as just another executive, but as a child of God.

When Peter reached this position of incredible authority, he had reached a beautiful and exhilarating point in his life. This was a high point. But, from here on the whole tone of his maturing process was going to change. Peter wasn't ready to handle it. Peter, like many of us, again had to come to the end of himself before Christ could take him deeper.

Chapter 4

OBSTACLES TO MATURITY

Everyone of us who wants to know the secret of being filled by Christ and becoming an effective, fruitful Christian has to go through an agonizing progression of thrilling blessings and heartbreaking failures. There is no way to speed up the process. There is no way to learn obedience and trust without Christ having to deal with us. We are so stubborn, so rebellious, so self-confident that the Lord has to teach us to face ourselves, not as others see us, but as He sees us. Only then do we realize in abject humility how much we need Him. We cannot change ourselves. We are too hampered by obstacles to maturity. Jesus Christ must deal with these obstacles to maturity and remove them one by one. When God allows the believer to go through troubles and problems, it is because He is trying to remove from our life those things that stand in the way of our growing up.

We have come a long way with Peter. We have watched him progress from his first encounter with Christ to the great moment when he learned about faith and walked on water. Then he learned about trusting the Word of God and accepting the hard sayings of Jesus. Finally we watched as he realized and testified that Christ is the Son of the living God and was rewarded with great authority and the keys of the kingdom.

Unfortunately, Peter had not yet met the obstacles which test the believer's faith and obedience. When he did meet them, he failed so dramatically that his behavior might suggest that he wasn't really a Christian in the first place.

THE FIRST OBSTACLE
Refusal to Take Up the Cross

This was the first obstacle Peter encountered that was so serious it prevented further growth. It is found in Matthew 16:21-27.

"From that time onward Jesus began to explain to his disciples that he would have to go to Jerusalem, and endure much suffering from the elders, chief priests and scribes, and finally be killed; and be raised to life again on the third day.

"Then Peter took him on one side and started to remonstrate with him over this. 'God bless you, Master! Nothing like this must happen to you!' Then Jesus turned round and said to Peter, 'Out of my way, Satan! . . . You stand right in my path, Peter, when you look at things from man's point of view and not from God's.'

"Then Jesus said to his disciples: 'If anyone wants to follow in my footsteps he must give up all right to himself, take up his cross and follow me. For the man who wants to save his life will lose it; but the man who loses his life for my sake will find it. For what good is it for a man to gain the whole world at the price of his own soul? What could a man offer to buy back his soul once he had lost it?

" 'For the Son of Man will come in the glory of his Father and in the company of his angels and then he will repay every man for what he has done.' "

The Unredeemed Mind

Not long before, the Lord Jesus made tremendous promises to Peter because of his confession of faith. Now Peter suddenly had the audacity to turn around and dictate to the Lord. The Lord was telling them about the cross. He was telling them how He would have to die—to shed blood for the redemption of the world. Peter, expressing great ignorance and arrogance, dared to contradict his Lord's teaching. Perhaps he felt his new authority gave him the right to question Christ.

Peter was not the first, nor will he be the last to tell Christ what is good and what isn't good. Many people do just that because they cannot accept certain things from the Bible. The doctrine of the blood of the cross is particularly offensive to unbelievers. They suggest that the cross is a carryover from an unsophisticated culture, and that today, to talk of dying on the cross and the shedding of blood is repulsive to a cultured and educated human being.

But it isn't repulsive to a cultured, educated person who recognizes the depth of his own depravity, his own self-centeredness and sin. Only when a man sees himself as God sees him does he realize that only in the blood of Christ can he find the hope he seeks.

Christ used this occasion to show that the gospel is diametrically opposed to unredeemed human nature. Romans 8:6-8 tells us that, "To set the mind on the flesh is death, but to set the mind on the Spirit is life and peace. For the mind that is set on the flesh is hostile to God; it does not submit to God's law, indeed it cannot; and those who are in the flesh cannot please God." (RSV)

The human mind, unredeemed, is hostile to the gospel. We can't stand the message of redemption through the blood until the Holy Spirit comes and takes over. The human mind rebels against the thought of the Son of God giving His blood on the cross. "Mankind can't be that bad," some people reason. "Surely there must be another way to God," and so on. We rebel against it just as Peter did.

Christ will not leave a Christian in error long. He uses our mistakes to continue our education. Christ met Peter head on at every turn. It must have been a shock to Peter because every time he said something

48

it seems it was the wrong thing. And all the time he had the best intentions at heart. When Peter objected to Christ's talking about the cross and His sacrifice, he might have expected a grateful response from Christ. After all, Peter was showing his love and protection of his Lord. But no, the Lord Jesus did not commend him. Instead He chastised Peter for thinking only as a man, and letting Satan influence him.

It must have stunned Peter to be rebuked so dramatically. Peter had not yet learned that he must die to self, to his own wishes, preferences, and opinions and to let Christ rule totally without contradiction and without opposition. Opposition to Christ and His redemptive work is Satan's sworn duty. No wonder Christ's response to Peter's concern was an uncompromising rebuke of Satan's influence on him.

Jesus spoke not only of His own death but He also taught that death is the doorway to life. He said, "If anyone wants to follow in my footsteps he must give up all right to himself, take up his cross and follow me."

Bearing the Cross

What is the cross? As I understand it, it is this. Every time the will of God clashes with my will, I choose His. Bearing one's cross does not mean tolerating an aggressive mother-in-law, or enduring a financial problem, troublesome as those things might be. It goes much deeper than that. When your self-will and your confident attitude cross the will of God, and you humbly choose to follow God's will, you have taken up the cross.

This is the hardest lesson for a Christian to learn. There are millions of Christians who are still babies spiritually because they have stopped at this obstacle and will not go any further. They cannot accept the cross of Jesus Christ.

When you surrender your will, and all that makes you proud and arrogant, to God, you have overcome a great obstacle to growth. But you must be willing to say, "Lord, everything I have—intellect, social standing, ability to make money—all this is a gift from you. You graciously gave me these abilities and I thank you for them, but, Lord, I want your will and your way in my life."

When you give up self, life begins to flow. Remember Galatians 2:20. "My present life is not that of the old 'I' but the living Christ within me. The bodily life I now live, I live believing in the Son of God, who loved me and sacrificed himself for me."

Overflowing Life

When a man finally comes to the cross where he actually chooses God's will against his own, he comes alive, and as the indwelling Christ begins to take over, his life begins to overflow. Jesus promised this in John 7:37,38 when He said, "If any man is thirsty, he can come to me and drink! The man who believes in me, as the scripture said, will have rivers of living water flowing from his inmost heart."

In other words, when a man comes to the end of himself and he says, "I am thirsty, I am needy, I don't have all that it takes," it is then that the Holy Spirit takes over and the water of life begins to flow. And when a man is Spirit filled, he is at peace with the Lord, and at peace with himself. He is not stiff, uptight, and self-centered. There is a way about him that says, "Jesus Christ is in control of this man's life."

Anyone can know if the Holy Spirit is flowing through him or if he is trying to do it on his own. There is a quietness, a peace, and a reality about a man or a woman within whom Christ is in control. This is the natural, normal state for the believer, and until the obstacles are removed which prevent a person from realizing full obedience to Christ, he will be an unfulfilled, restless, discontented Christian. There is no alternative to learning to take up the cross.

THE SECOND OBSTACLE
Uncontrolled Tongue

One of the signs that shows Christ is not in control of our lives is a loose tongue that says things which hurt people. Peter was guilty of this.

Matthew 17:2-8 tells us, "There [Jesus'] whole appearance changed before their eyes, his face shining like the sun and his clothes as white as light. Then

51

Moses and Elijah were seen talking to Jesus.

" 'Lord,' exclaimed Peter, 'it is wonderful for us to be here! If you like I could put up three shelters, one each for you and Moses and Elijah—'

"But while he was still talking a bright cloud over-shadowed them and a voice came out of the cloud: 'This is my dearly loved Son in whom I am well pleased. Listen to him!'

"When they heard this voice the disciples fell on their faces, overcome with fear. Then Jesus came up to them and touched them. 'Get up and don't be frightened,' he said. And as they raised their eyes there was no one to be seen but Jesus himself."

Here was a wonderful scene to witness—the Son of God transfigured like He is going to be in glory. Here were Moses and Elijah. They were talking about the death of Christ on the cross; talking about the redemption that was going to take place in Jerusalem; talking about the most solemn and momentous event of history—the Son of God dying for the sins of mankind. This was a glorious revelation of the presence of God.

But Peter, with an uncontrolled tongue, dared again to interrupt his Lord. "Lord, it is wonderful for us to be here! If you like I could put up three shelters, one each for you and Moses and Elijah!" Here was the "I" coming to the fore. Peter offered to handle all the details and erect three monuments. But, before he was through with his little speech, God interrupted. A bright cloud came and covered them and the voice of the Father said, "This is my dearly loved Son in whom I am well pleased. Listen to him!" The Father was saying, "Peter, be still. This is the Son of God. Keep quiet and listen to Him."

We are all guilty of this. We take so little time to listen to God. We are so arrogant, so self-confident. We think so much of our opinions. Peter was sincere and that must have made God's rebuke doubly shocking. Many Christians suffer with the same affliction: sincere ignorance. We mean right. We want to please the Lord, and yet everything we do seems to bring rebuke instead of blessing. Uncrucified pride is what gets us in trouble, and sometimes Christ is forced to use strong tactics to break through it.

Shock Treatment

Perhaps it was a little harsh on the part of the Lord to first call Peter Satan, and then later to tell him to be still. But sometimes shock treatment is what we need, and it is a good method if it is done in love. There are two men in my life, each one of whom has been used of God to deal me tremendous blows, but they were used of God to straighten out my life.

One of them is Ray Stedman. Through him God brought me to the United States. I knew he loved me like a son. I've seen in this man more of the character and temperament of Jesus Christ than any man I've ever met and I've seen him under all kinds of stress and pressure.

When I first arrived, I wanted to serve Christ. I was sincere like Peter, but I was far removed from knowing about the indwelling Christ. I did not understand that it was not Luis Palau, but Christ in me who had to do the job. Like every young man who wants to serve Christ, I thought quite a bit of myself. I had been educated in British schools, and in the Cambridge program and felt a great sense of pride when I preached and gave little messages. I felt I knew what I was talking about.

One day I sat down with Ray Stedman to talk about something left unsettled in Argentina. He said to me, "Luis, you had better settle that thing." I said, "Don't worry. When I get back home, I'll talk to a few people and get out of it." Then he said to me, "Yes, you have a fast tongue. And one of these days you are going to talk yourself right into hell with that same tongue. You're going to talk yourself into such a problem that nobody will be able to get you out."

That was a blow! But then he went on, very lovingly and said, "Luis, you are so proud and cocky that it oozes out of your pores and you don't even realize it!" When someone says that and he is not kidding, you know it is God's voice. I knew it. There was no need for confirmation. My friend was right.

That was the beginning of a turn for me. Proverbs 27:6 says, "Faithful are the wounds of a friend; but the kisses of an enemy are deceitful" (*KJV*). When someone really loves you and he sees weaknesses in you, he's going to put his arm around you and let you have it. Fortunate is the man who has such friends.

When I got married only a few months later, my wife and I were sent to Detroit, Michigan, for some studies in psychology. The Lord had another lesson waiting for me there. I call this the final "bringing me to the cross once and for all" blow.

We were missionary interns working at a Baptist church. I was supposed to help the pastor. They gave us lodging in the attic of the home of a woman who was aging and a bit eccentric. She refused to give us a key and would suddenly walk into the room whenever she pleased. We had been married just three weeks and young married couples like their privacy. I became so angry about the situation that instead of going to the director of the missionary internship program, I wrote to the director of Overseas Crusades. I threatened to leave the internship program and said that if he wanted to throw me out of Overseas Crusades he could go right ahead, but to get me out of that attic!

Overseas Crusades, of course, wrote immediately to Fred Renich, the director of our internship program, and said, "What are you doing to this young couple? We sent them to you to train and you put them in an impossible situation. . . !"

Mr. Renich acted quickly. However, he saw beyond my actions to the arrogance that my actions exhibited and my lack of humility and Christian character. He called me in and said, "Luis, I have a letter here telling me to get you out of that attic. You will be out of the apartment by tomorrow. But I'd like to ask why you didn't come to me instead of writing to your director?"

I said, "I wanted to be sure I'd get action."

"The line of authority would be through me," he

said. "This way you made me look like a clown in front of your director. It hurt me." He went on. "Let me tell you something. If you look at your wife, Pat, you will notice that she is quiet, easy-going, and pliable. If you don't let Christ take over in your life, you are going to step all over her all through your life. You are going to crush her, and you will never even know it. Think back on your life. I'm willing to bet you, Luis, that all along the pathway of your life are the skeletons of people that you have stepped on and hurt because of your aggressive temperament. And you don't even know it."

I returned to my attic somewhat stunned. Everything he had said was accurate. I thought over my life and remembered a number of people whom I had cruelly injured with my pride and self-righteousness. I remembered how many Sunday School teachers just dropped out of the Sunday School because of my demands as superintendent. I thought I was being rigorous and disciplined in my expectations, but realized now that I was just stepping on them in my egotism and pride without knowing it.

The shock treatment that Jesus Christ gave to Peter was necessary to show him his real self and make him realize that in and of himself, he was an arrogant and useless character.

THE THIRD OBSTACLE
Blight of Legalism

Grace takes precedence over the law, and Jesus

56

in His dealings with Peter displayed the graciousness and love we are to extend to others in Jesus' name. Christ gave an example of this in Matthew 18:21,22 when He told Peter that there is no limit to the number of times he must forgive a brother who has sinned against him.

THE FOURTH OBSTACLE
Tendency to Compare

The Lord rebuked the rich and Peter said, "That's right, Lord. Let them have it. I have left everything to follow you. What will I get in the kingdom?" Peter felt, that in comparison to others, he deserved a reward for his spirituality.

Peter refused to understand that he couldn't have his own way and God's will at the same time. He couldn't let go of self and let Christ be all. All the lessons that Peter learned, the lessons that God used Stedman and Renich to teach me, were God's way of telling us that Christ must have preeminence in our lives.

Let Him control you and you will be the kind of man you want to be—the kind of man God wants you to be. Praise God for shock treatments!

Chapter 5

MORE OBSTACLES...

Jesus Christ said in the Gospel of John, chapter 10, verse 10, "I came to bring them life, and far more life than before." Christ wants every man and woman to live an abundant life, a joyful life, a truthful life, a happy life. When Jesus Christ takes hold of a man, His objective is, as soon as possible, to get him to grow up, to make him a real man. Christ came so that we could be conformed to the image of God's Son. He wants to make us over with the character of His Son, Jesus Christ. That is His objective.

An often-quoted promise occurs in Philippians 1:6. "I feel sure that the one who has begun his good work in you will go on developing it until the day of Jesus Christ." This is a great comfort and promise for every believer. When Christ takes over in a life, He will finish the job. What He started, He will finish.

If He came all the way to earth, became a man, and let Himself be crucified to be able to forgive our past and cleanse our lives, don't you think He plans to finish the job? Of course He does! He is not going to start something and then let go. It cost Him too much.

In Peter we see a man in the process of maturing. He is in the process of being brought to completion. Every one of our lives is in that process. The measure of how far we have come depends, however, on how willing we have been to let the indwelling Christ take over our lives. Our responsibility is to cooperate with Him by willingly letting Him have His way in our lives. This cooperation was difficult for one as stubborn as Peter. It took Jesus Christ many months before He could bring him to a place of obedience. It was necessary to shock Peter out of his self-will. But such shocks caused a healthy breakdown of his old patterns of living. With each new obstacle to maturity he encountered, Peter learned a greater degree and depth of obedience to his Master. Christ used Peter's failures to teach him, and teach us, how to walk with God. Peter is an excellent example for studying this process because he failed so dramatically, and so often.

THE FIFTH OBSTACLE
Unrecognized Defilement

In John 13:4-11 we read that Jesus washed His disciples' feet. The situation became a vehicle for the instruction of several truths, one of which was the danger of unrecognized defilement. Peter did not recognize that he was defiled and needed cleansing.

In the Middle East, there were no paved roads and a lot of dust. When a person went to a dinner or a party, he was expected to bathe before setting out. But on the walk from his home to the host's house, the guest would get his feet dirty. Dusty feet were an unpleasant accompaniment for a dinner, especially since the diners did not sit at a table but rather reclined on a couch. So, the custom was for a servant of the host to wash the guest's feet.

On this occasion, Christ and His disciples had come together for the Lord's Supper, the final Passover. They had no slaves; no one to wash each other's feet. So, the Lord Jesus Himself took off His outer clothing, rolled up His sleeves, got a basin of water, and stooped before them to wash their feet.

They all had dust on their feet. They were all defiled. But when He came to Peter, Peter objected to having his feet washed. We are told that Peter said, " 'You must never wash my feet!'

" 'Unless you let me wash you, Peter,' replied Jesus, 'you cannot share my lot.'

" 'Then,' returned Simon Peter, 'please—not just my feet but my hands and my face as well!' " (See John 13:8,9.)

Peter was sincere in his concern that Christ not stoop to wash his feet. Here was a man with defiled feet, but he wasn't aware of his need, or if he was aware, he didn't want Christ to remedy it.

It is a tremendous obstacle to maturity when we

think that we are all right—that we don't need this daily cleansing by the Word of God and by the blood of Jesus Christ. There are thousands of Christians who believe that they are all right. They feel, perhaps, that new Christians or ex-drug addicts might have to stay close to the Lord because the old temptations will trouble them, but overlook the fact that every believer needs to have his feet washed daily.

Defiant Heart

Not only was Peter defiled but he had a defiant heart. Contamination alone would not trouble the Lord. He knows each one of our lives and is not shaken by your contamination or mine. What troubled the Lord was Peter's defiant heart. When Peter objected to having his feet washed, Jesus responded with a strong statement. "Unless you let me wash you, Peter, you cannot share my lot." What did the Lord mean? He knew of Peter's love and commitment and sincerity.

What Peter didn't know and had to learn was that if Christ was not permitted to cleanse him from daily defilement, from the impurities of mind, heart, and soul which accrued as he went through the world, he could have no part in friendship with Christ. There could be no fruitfulness because a contaminated vessel cannot hold or dispense blessing.

Every day the believer has to come back gladly to the feet of Jesus Christ and be cleansed and refreshed. The interesting thing about this episode is that Peter, in spite of his rebellion, had an honest heart, for when the Lord Jesus said that Peter couldn't share His lot if he didn't get washed. Peter urgently exclaimed, "Then, please—not just my feet but my hands and my face as well!" He had a sincere heart. He had no intention of breaking away from the Lord, and the possibility alarmed him. As usual, he didn't see himself as he ought to. So, just to make sure that he would retain his part with Christ, he requested an entire bath if that is what the Lord required. Peter may have been stubborn, but his inner heart was honest, and it is by our hearts that God judges us.

Scripture is full of examples of such people. King David made many mistakes. He committed tremendous sins. He committed adultery with one of his soldier's wives, then had the soldier killed to cover up for the child that was coming. And yet, God says about David, "I have found David, the Son of Jesse, a man after my own heart" (Acts 13:22). Why? Because man looks on the outward appearance, but God looks on the heart. God can handle our temptations and failures if our hearts are willing to continue trusting Him. God knows the failings of His saints because there has never been one yet who was not sorely tempted by something.

I have met people who claim that they don't have a problem with temptation. They are covering up, or they are so out of touch with Christ that they don't feel their need. I've met people who resent discussing problems about sexual temptations. These people sometimes feel that once we are Christians we don't have a problem with that. Either such people are deluded, or kidding, or I am just different. All the way through life, from youth to old age, a normal human being is continually tempted.

I remember meeting an 85-year-old doctor who was a missionary in Argentina, a very distinguished man of God. I was seventeen and very impressed with him. One day he came to our home, as he did once in a while, and took me off to the living room alone to talk with me. I was having all the normal struggles and temptations of an adolescent and fervently longed for the day when I would be Godly enough not to be troubled by them. In those days, I thought that only young people had sexual temptations and that the moment you married temptation was gone. A lot of people still like to think that. He seemed so righteous and pure that I was stunned when, in the course of our conversation, he admitted honestly to still being tempted sexually. It was an eye-opening talk for me. Christians constantly face temptation but God has provided help for us.

Resisting Temptation

There are three recourses for us when we are tempted. First we can take comfort in *the mind of Christ*. First Corinthians 2:16 tells us that the mind of Christ is now ours. If by faith we appropriate His indwelling presence, we can keep our thinking straight. It doesn't eliminate the temptation, but it helps us to keep our thinking consistent with what Christ wills.

Secondly, *the indwelling power of the Holy Spirit* helps us to implement the thinking of the mind of Christ.

Thirdly, we have to have *the right kind of input*. The Bible says in Philippians 4:8,9, "Here is a last piece of advice. If you believe in goodness and if you value the approval of God, fix your minds on whatever is true and honorable and just and pure and lovely and praiseworthy. Model your conduct on what you have learned from me, on what I have told you and shown you, and you will find that the God of peace will be with you." What we entertain in our minds affects our whole personality. Temptation never goes away, not even for the holiest of men. But there is power to overcome impurity of mind and the passions that are misdirected. It is the indwelling power of the Holy Spirit.

THE SIXTH OBSTACLE
Not Accepting the Warnings of Scripture

"Simon Peter said to him, 'Lord, where are you going?'

" 'I am going,' replied Jesus, 'where you cannot follow me now, though you will follow me later.'

" 'Lord, why can't I follow you now?' said Peter. 'I would lay down my life for you!'

" 'Would you lay down your life for me?' replied Jesus. 'Believe me, you will disown me three times before the cock crows!' " John 13:36,37.

Here is a warning that the Lord Jesus was gra-

ciously giving to Peter. Scripture repeatedly warns
believers about the obstacles and the problems of
the Christian life and gives us guidelines on how to
handle ourselves. We are told to be especially cautious
when we feel most confident, because that is when
we are most likely to be caught off guard. But, unless
we accept the warnings, we are candidates for failure.
In Luke 22:31-34 Peter again ignores the importance
of a warning of Scripture.

" 'Oh, Simon, Simon, do you know that Satan has
asked to have you all to sift like wheat?—But I have
prayed for you that you may not lose your faith.
Yes, when you have turned back to me, you must
strengthen these brothers of yours.'

"Peter said to him,

" 'Lord, I am ready to go to prison, or even to
die with you!'

" 'I tell you, Peter,' returned Jesus, 'before the cock
crows today you will deny three times that you know
me!' "

In spite of the fact that Christ told Peter that Satan
had asked to trouble them, Peter couldn't take such
warnings seriously. He still didn't know himself. He
sincerely believed that he was ready to go to prison
and to death for Christ. He insisted that even if all
the others denied Christ, he would remain faithful.

Know Satan Is Real

Scripture warns us that Satan is a real enemy. He
is not a story to frighten kids. He isn't a threat just

to keep bad people in line. Satan is alive and active. Look around and see if Satan hasn't sifted families that you know. Maybe he has disrupted your own family. It is dangerous not to take seriously the warnings of Scripture about the power of Satan, and about the need to trust Christ's indwelling power day by day, moment by moment. If you think you can ignore the warnings of Scripture and avoid Satan's influence you are taking a dangerous chance. The most dedicated and disciplined people sometimes are the very ones who fall flat. We don't take the warnings of Scripture seriously enough. As a result, new converts get overconfident and think that perhaps Christianity is not as difficult as the Bible suggests. They see our complacency and are fooled by Satan. We become severe stumbling blocks to new Christians who look to us for example.

A friend of mine has a saying that goes like this, "Woe to the man who has to learn principles at a time of crisis." That is good advice. You have to learn the principles of the Scriptures before the crisis strikes so you know where you stand. Ephesians 6:10-20 tells us to prepare ahead so we will be able to stand in the evil day. It tells us about Satan's attacks and about the evil day. Evil days come and go, but we can remain strong.

Remember when Jesus was tempted, Scripture says, Satan left Him for a season—a little while. Satan attacks people unexpectedly in waves and then lets them breathe a bit, then attacks again. To the prepared Christian, Satan's attacks are futile. The believer is standing on the promises of the indwelling

Jesus Christ, and that is sufficient. You can stand if you take Satan seriously and are prepared. If you do not, you are in trouble.

Use Spiritual Weapons

Another obstacle to maturity that the Christian must face is an interesting one—*carnal weapons*. In Luke 22:35-38, Jesus was teaching His disciples saying, "That time when I sent you out without any purse or wallet or shoes—did you find you needed anything?'

" 'No, not a thing,' they replied.

" 'But now,' Jesus continued, 'if you have a purse or wallet, take it with you, and if you have no sword, sell your coat and buy one! for I tell you that this scripture must be fulfilled in me—

" 'And he was reckoned with transgressors.

So comes the end of what they wrote about me.'

Then the disciples said,

'Lord, look, here are two swords.'

And Jesus returned,

'That is enough.' "

Then in John 18:10,11 we are told that while the soldiers were taking the Lord Jesus prisoner, "Simon Peter, who had a sword, drew it and slashed at the High Priest's servant, cutting off his right ear. (The servant's name was Malchus.) But Jesus said to Peter, 'Put your sword back into its sheath. Am I not to drink the cup the Father has given me?' "

The Lord seems to have set Peter up for this one.

Until now, all the crises between Peter and the Lord Jesus had been of Peter's own making. Jesus had said if you don't have a sword, buy one. And Peter, in zealous obedience, happily got a sword. He thought perhaps that now that the showdown was coming, he could show everyone and show Christ how faithful he was and how much he loved Jesus. Perhaps he felt he could, with his actions in defense of Christ, redeem his past errors. Whatever Peter's motivation, it is interesting to note that in his dramatic attack all he managed to do was cut off one fellow's ear.

Peter probably expected the Lord Jesus to commend him for his faithfulness. Instead he was told to put his sword away while Jesus repaired the damage. It seems that in everything Peter did, he was reproved, warned, rebuked, and criticized by Christ. But he must have been completely shocked by this event. His Lord was about to be crucified and Jesus called it, "My Father's cup." Peter couldn't understand why he couldn't defend his Lord in the face of death. Then Jesus explained, "I could call for a hundred thousand angels and they could defend me." Dear Peter with all his zeal, was not needed. His weapon was nothing compared to Christ's weapon of power.

When we find ourselves desperate and we are not walking in the indwelling power of Jesus Christ, we all have the tendency to begin to use a carnal weapon of our own making. It can be something we studied in college, some book we just finished reading, or something that we heard someone say. Instead of trusting the power of almighty God who has come to dwell within through the resurrected Christ, we gather together ineffectual swords and hack away under our own power. But in the spiritual warfare, only spiritual weapons will do. Paul tells us even though we live in the flesh, we don't operate after the flesh. "The very weapons we use are not those of human warfare but powerful in God's warfare for the destruction of the enemy's strongholds. Our battle is to bring down every deceptive fantasy and every imposing defense that men erect against the true knowledge of God" (2 Cor. 10:4,5).

We planned a crusade in Costa Rica for February of 1972. We thought everything was going to go fantastically well, but when we got there, we discovered that certain leaders in the country suddenly had turned against mass evangelism. They had spread the word during the month of preparation that mass evangelism didn't produce any results; that it was old fashioned; that all this saving of souls was unimportant compared to the great social issues of our day. Some of the theologians, very famous Latin-American men, insisted that this was old-fashioned and that leading people to Christ would do nothing for the country and they were not going to waste their time or their money on a crusade to bring people to Christ.

I had to kneel day after day during the first week of the four-week crusade and say to the Lord, "Thank you for bringing us here. Thank you that we know you are in control of this crusade. We don't want to take it upon ourselves. We want to show your power." It was a tremendous temptation to use carnal weapons and let the liberals have it from the pulpit.

70

It was a hard temptation to control, but we knew that the Lord could show His power and relevance in the world today much better than we could. The result of our faith was thrilling. Of all the crusades we've ever had, the Costa Rica crusade produced more evidence of obvious conversions and results than any other.

More people stayed in the churches; more letters were written than you can imagine. The Christian radio station in that town got thousands of phone calls demanding that they replay the crusade sermons every morning. Some people even put ads in the newspaper calling upon the station to play the same crusade messages every evening. They broadcasted them for three months, twice a day, at public request.

We couldn't have done that. But the people did it. We didn't suggest that they do it. They did it on their own. Now Costa Rica knows that the gospel does have power to change people's lives. But it was God who moved the people to overcome the obstacles, not us.

When, as a Christian, you feel tempted to use carnal weapons, recognize it as an obstacle to maturity. Say, "No, Lord. It would feel good to do it. But, Lord, I know it would be wrong. It would dishonor you, and I want *your* power to do it."

Surrender Your Will

After Christ rebuked Peter for drawing his sword, the Bible tells us that Christ was led away and Peter followed. Peter had not yet experienced the lowest point of his life, the final blow.

"Then they arrested him and marched him off to the High Priest's house. Peter followed at a distance, and sat down among some people who had lighted a fire in the middle of the courtyard and were sitting round it. A maidservant saw him sitting there in the firelight, peered into his face and said, 'This man was with him, too.' But he denied it and said, 'I don't know him, girl!'

"A few minutes later someone else noticed Peter, and said, 'You're one of these men too.' But Peter said, 'Man, I am not!'

"Then about an hour later someone else insisted, 'I am convinced this fellow was with him. Why, he is a Galilean!'

" 'Man,' returned Peter, 'I don't know what you're talking about.' And immediately, while he was still speaking, the cock crew. The Lord turned his head and looked straight at Peter, into whose mind flashed the words that the Lord had said to him . . . 'You will disown me three times before the cock crows today.' And he went outside and wept bitterly" (Luke 22:54-62).

Peter made a critical error in defending himself. In John 12:24,25 Jesus said, "I tell you truly that unless a grain of wheat falls into the earth and dies, it remains a single grain of wheat; but if it dies, it brings a good harvest. The man who loves his own life will destroy it, and the man who hates his life in this world will preserve it for eternal life."

There are thousands of Christian men and women

who are useless to the cause of Christ. They belong to Christ, but are not overflowing with Christ because they're trying to save their own lives. They are always protecting themselves, always covering for themselves, always justifying themselves, always explaining why they can't do this or that. We must be willing to give up our will for His, our lives for His life through us. That is taking up the cross.

In this final crisis Peter failed totally and irrevocably. Peter, who had only a few hours before promised to go to jail and even die for Christ if necessary, denied he ever even knew the Man. And so important was it to Peter to remove himself from all complicity that he denied knowing his Master with oaths and curses to a lowly maid whose opinions really posed no real danger for him.

It is painful to see Peter pushed all the way to total denial. It wasn't necessary. Certainly God didn't want that. The Lord doesn't want us to suffer the logical consequences of our weaknesses. He would rather we turned them over to Him long before they get us into critical difficulties.

Not long ago a lady told me of her tragic experience. "We were Christian workers with children. We were dedicated to Christ and had won many children to the Lord. Our dedication was a source of self-pride, of self-satisfaction. But, we had to be brought to our senses. You know what did it? The death of our baby. When that happened, we realized how enchanted with ourselves we were. When I lost my child, we realized our work was a privilege for God. Serving Him, being alive, being a Christian, and winning children for

Christ was a blessed responsibility. Our lives have really been filled with the Spirit since that time."

Does God want us to have to go through all that pain? I don't think so. But often we bring it upon ourselves when we refuse to go the way He asks us to go. The Lord loves us. He is very patient and gracious. But you can't play games with God. Eventually if you resist His guidance and resist His will, He is going to let you go all the way in your willful direction, whatever it happens to be. For some it may be immorality, for others a life-sapping drug habit, for still others emotional break-down. The stakes are high when dealing with eternal values.

Isn't it interesting that the Lord looked at Peter. This is a very touching incident to me. The Lord was surrounded by His accusers while Peter was denying Him about fifty yards away. When Peter denied Him and the cock crowed, the Lord Jesus took time to look at Peter. Christ didn't speak or even make any signal, just looked at him. It must have been quite a look because Peter went out and wept bitterly. The Lord Jesus said volumes to Peter in that look, and, for a heartbroken Peter, all Christ's words and warnings fell into place. What months of teaching had failed to do, a quiet look accomplished in a moment.

Suddenly Peter saw himself. He saw it all, and was repentant. Imagine this sensitive, crushed man, alone, walking in the mountains of Jerusalem wrenched with weeping. His Lord had been taken, the disciples scattered, and he was alone with his terrible guilt and his Master's words echoing in his head.

It is fortunate in some ways that Scripture does not record details of Peter's pain, for few people in history must have suffered so terrible a conclusion to such great anticipations.

Chapter 6

EXIT SIMON THE DISCIPLE; ENTER PETER THE APOSTLE

What does God want from us, really? What is His goal as He tests our faith, permits great obstacles to hinder our growth, and allows defeat and pain to overwhelm us? What did Peter gain from his sometimes thrilling, but often agonizing experience of knowing Jesus?

In John 21:1-19 we read of Peter's next encounter with Jesus. If he has been changed Scripture will record it. Jesus had already been crucified, had risen from the grave, and had been witnessed by some of the disciples.

"Later on, Jesus showed himself again to his disciples on the shore of Lake Tiberias, and he did it in this way. Simon Peter, Thomas (called the twin), Nathanael from Cana of Galilee, the sons of Zebedee and two other disciples were together, when Simon Peter said, 'I'm going fishing.'

"'All right,' they replied, 'we'll go with you.'

"So they went out and got into the boat and during the night caught nothing at all. But just as dawn began to break, Jesus stood there on the beach, although the disciples had no idea that it was Jesus. 'Have you caught anything, lads?' Jesus called out to them.

" 'No,' they replied.

" 'Throw the net on the right side of the boat,' said Jesus, 'and you'll have a catch.'

"So they threw out the net and found that they were now not strong enough to pull it in because it was so full of fish! At this, the disciple that Jesus loved said to Peter, 'It is the Lord!'

"Hearing this, Peter slipped on his clothes, for he had been naked, and plunged into the sea. The other disciples followed in the boat, for they were only about a hundred yards from the shore, dragging in the net full of fish. When they had landed, they saw that a charcoal fire was burning, with a fish placed on it, and some bread. Jesus said to them, 'Bring me some of the fish you've just caught.'

"So Simon Peter got into the boat and hauled the net ashore full of large fish, one hundred and fifty-three altogether. But in spite of the large number the net was not torn.

"Then Jesus said to them, 'Come and have your breakfast.'

"None of the disciples dared to ask him who he was; they knew it was the Lord.

"Jesus went and took the bread and gave it to them and gave them all fish as well. This is already the third time that Jesus showed himself to his disciples after his resurrection from the dead.

"When they had finished breakfast Jesus said to Simon Peter, 'Simon, son of John, do you love me more than these others?'

" 'Yes, Lord,' he replied, 'you know that I am your friend.'

" 'Then feed my lambs,' returned Jesus. Then he said for the second time, 'Simon, son of John, do you love me?'

" 'Yes, Lord,' returned Peter. 'You know that I am your friend.'

" 'Then care for my sheep,' replied Jesus. Then for the third time, Jesus spoke to him and said, 'Simon, son of John, *are* you my friend?'

"Peter was deeply hurt because Jesus' third question to him was 'Are you my friend?' and he said: 'Lord, you know everything. You know that I am your friend!'

" 'Then feed my sheep,' Jesus said to him. 'I tell you truly, Peter, that when you were younger, you used to dress yourself and go where you liked, but when you are an old man, you are going to stretch out your hands and someone else will dress you and take you where you do not want to go.' [He said this to show the kind of death by which Peter was going to honor God.]

"Then Jesus said to him, 'You must follow me.' "

What Jesus Christ was trying to do with Peter was to bring him under the control of the indwelling Son of God, the living resurrected Christ. God is not trying to make us religious. He is not trying to make us toe the line. He is not trying to make us dedicated, bitter, tense, self-sufficient people; not at all. He is trying to bring us into such a relationship with Him that we shall be controlled by Him; happy, joyful, free, fruitful—real men and women. He doesn't expect us to be perfect, but He does expect us to learn control. He doesn't expect sinlessness, but He does expect maturity. And He does not expect us to do this alone. He is the One who has begun the work in us, and He has promised that He will finish it.

Controlled at Last

God continued to work with Peter until his dying day, and accomplished great things through him.

In the above passage, Peter was called and commissioned once again. Peter must have experienced great confusion at that. His denial had been so severe, his cursing and swearing so out of order that he must surely have felt that Christ was through with him. He had, in fact, gone back to fishing. But it wasn't all over for him in spite of what he may have felt, and in spite of what he had done.

Many Christians at times have believed that what they did last week, or last month, or a few years ago, was so bad they do not deserve to have anything more to do with the Lord. Some people, when overwhelmed by guilt, believe they have sinned against the Holy Spirit and believe there is no more hope. But, the very fact that a Christian is experiencing such deep concern is proof that the living God is still at work in his life and that He is calling the believer to Himself.

Peter was the first disciple Christ appeared to after His resurrection. First Corinthians 15:5 says He appeared first to Cephas (Peter). It is interesting that after He had come out of the grave, the Lord Jesus personally went looking for Peter. Jesus, more than anyone else, certainly knew how Peter must have suffered at the cross, and so He looked for him first after the Resurrection. Then the Lord allowed Peter to go back to fishing so that He could remind him of his original calling. When He met Peter the first time, the situation was identical. They were fishing, they had caught nothing, and the Lord stepped into their lives and everything was changed. Once again when Peter discovered the barrenness of self-effort, the Lord showed up and gave him a promise even better than the first one.

When Jesus said to Simon Peter, "Simon, son of John, do you love me more than these others?" Jesus was using the Greek word *agape* meaning divine love—that perfect sacrificial love that only God can give us. When Peter replied with "Yes, Lord, you know that I am your friend," Peter didn't use *agape*. He used *phileo* which means friend. The Lord was asking Peter if he loved Him with that perfect love that he vowed when he promised to go to prison or die for Christ. And Peter could only admit to a great affection, a friendship for Christ. A second time, Jesus asked Peter if Peter loved Him with that divine love, and a second time Peter could only admit to friendship.

The third time, Jesus asked a different question. "Simon, son of John, *are* you my friend?" In other

81

words, Jesus was asking, "If you are claiming to feel great affection and friendship toward me, can I rely on that claim; do you really mean, this time, what you are saying to me?" No wonder Peter was deeply hurt with the last question. With it Christ recalled for Peter the pain and grief Peter had felt at betraying Christ after promising sacrificial—agape—love. And Peter, who had finally learned his lesson beautifully and had seen himself so accurately at last, realized that he was incapable of promising anything beyond friendship.

There was a new honesty in Peter. He no longer pretended what he had not found the strength to give. Pretense was gone; arrogance was gone. No longer did Peter dare to suggest that he knew more than the Lord. The last time Jesus asked His question He met Peter at Peter's own level. He was saying, "All right, Peter, are you *really* my friend? Do you have *phileo* love for me?" And Peter for the first time responded wholly and honestly to the question asked, "Lord, you know everything. You know that I am your friend!" Christ changed His question for Peter. He did not demand more of Peter than Peter could give. But Peter was, in fact, giving all that Christ desires from a believer—an honest, contrite, and humble heart.

It is hard for a man to wholly accept the fact that Jesus Christ knows everything; that Scripture is absolutely perfect; that questioning Scripture in unbelief is not a sign of intellectual maturity, but a sign of inner rebellion and pride. Few people have gone through what Peter did before learning this, but most

Christians struggle with some aspect of these questions from time to time. Once Peter was honest enough to confess that he didn't even trust his own love toward the Lord, then the Lord said to him, "Peter, feed my lambs, tend my lambs, feed my sheep." Christ gave Peter a new commission.

Empowered by the Holy Spirit

Every Christian should study Acts 2. Peter was not only called back and commissioned once again, but he was empowered by the Holy Spirit and sent out as a leader of the budding Church. Until now, all previous commissions were promises that Peter couldn't fulfill. He had to mature first; he had to grow into his commission. The Lord had promised Peter that he would grow to be so different that he would be a rock, and the Lord keeps His promises. But it wasn't until Pentecost, when the Holy Spirit of God came and once and for all formed the real Church, the body of Christ indwelt by the Holy Spirit, that Peter began to become the kind of man that the Lord had in mind for him; the kind of man He saw in Peter when He met him that day years before by Caesarea and called him to follow.

How far along have you come in your Christian walk? How many months or years ago has it been since Jesus Christ took over in your life? How much of the old ways have begun to be relegated to the past and how much of the new maturity has been coming to the fore?

How much of the Peter side of you can your wife see in the home? How much of the Peter can your children see in you as you talk and function in the family? In the church, are you a Simon or a Peter? Are you a loud, opinionated, boastful, self-sufficient church member? Or are you a fruitful, gracious, Christ-controlled man or woman. Have you learned to see yourself as Christ sees you—or even as others see you?

Have you grown to maturity in Christ whatever your age? There is a difference between growing up and just growing older. There are a lot of people who have grown old who have never grown up. Have you grown up in Jesus Christ? Can you say, honestly, "I have a long way to go, but by God's grace I'm not where I was, nor am I where I shall be, but, bless God, I'm with Him!"

It should be emphasized that when Peter reached the fulness of the Spirit of Pentecost, he was not perfect, but he was controlled. He was not sinless, but he was growing and maturing and he did so for the rest of his days. Isn't that the goal of every Christian? Isn't that where we want to be? We can't expect perfection this side of heaven because He said we cannot expect completion until the day of Jesus Christ. He has to work with each one of us until He returns. Peter did not become perfect, but he was controlled by the indwelling Christ. He was not sinless, but he was growing and maturing. And so dynamic was his life and his story that Peter, even today, glorifies God whenever we read about him. Study his epistles, look at his life, and you see a weak man, who, when he came face to face with Jesus Christ, is still bearing fruit two thousand years after his death.

If the Lord doesn't return in this generation wouldn't it be great if, when we have died, years from now people would still remember and learn something of Jesus Christ through our lives?

Saint Augustine was such a person. He was born in A.D. 354, but his life is still speaking to believers. He was a man who lived under the control of Christ in spite of weaknesses; and God is still speaking through him to Christians today.

Martin Luther was born in 1483 and God used him to change the history of the Christian church. Today, almost five hundred years after his death, God is still speaking to believers through his example of courage and conviction.

John Calvin was born in 1509 and generations later, God speaks to Christians through his commitment.

There are many other quiet people whose lives are still speaking God's message and blessing and promises today. What will your life show twenty years from now, one hundred, five hundred? How will people remember your life?

A friend told me that he went to see the place where Peter and Paul walked. Tradition says that Peter, when he was taken out to be crucified for his faith, requested that they crucify him upside down: "Because," he said, "I am not worthy to be crucified the same way that my Saviour died." This is not recorded in the Bible, but it sounds very much like Peter. And Christ did give him a hint of how he would die in John 21:18,19 which suggests crucifixion.

Paul said in Galatians 2:20, "As far as the Law is concerned I may consider that I died on the cross with Christ. And my present life is not that of the old 'I,' but the living Christ within me. The bodily life I now live, I live believing in the Son of God, who loved me and sacrificed himself for me."

When I discovered that simple secret, my whole life was transformed. How I thank God for the men God used to put His finger on my life until it hurt. The pain of seeing myself honestly brought me to reality. I learned that it was not what I was going to do for God, but what Christ was going to do through me that counted.

Simon Versus Peter

The whole purpose of Christ's dealings with Peter was not to squelch him and crush him. The whole point was to pick him up and make him live; to make Simon Peter one of the greatest men in all history. The point was to get Peter out of the way and let Christ take control of Peter's life. And from that day of Pentecost, Peter was not perfect, but the savor, the flavor, the perfume of Jesus Christ comes out through his life. We can even smell His perfume as we study his life today.

The Christ who made Peter who he was is the same wonderful Christ that lives in you and in me. And all He wants from us is that we be available to Him. All He asks is to take over. Just let Him take over and see what He can do through you.

Peter's life raises important issues for each Christian struggling to follow Christ. Where are you in the light of God's promises and God's purposes for you? Is God still dealing with you, or have you resisted His voice so long that you are so far away you can't hear His voice any more at all? Have you gone back to fishing while the Lord has been calling you from the shore? If so, dive into the water and swim quickly to Jesus and listen to His renewed call and commission. If you do, you will be able to say, "The bodily life I now live, I live believing in the Son of God, who loved me and sacrificed himself for me."

This is the heart of the gospel. The cross is the foundation, but the heart is the living Christ dwelling in us and living His life through us.